25
Totally Awesome & Totally Easy
Bulletin Boards

By Michael Gravois

SCHOLASTIC
PROFESSIONAL BOOKS

New York • Toronto • London • Auckland • Sydney
Mexico City • New Delhi • Hong Kong

Dedication

To Mrs. Wattigny, Mrs. Pinoges, Mrs. Ponstein,
Mrs. Boquet, Mrs. Cutrer, Mrs. Gaudet,
Mrs. Trosclair, Mrs. Capron, and Miss Stierwald

Interior design by Sydney Wright
Cover design by Jaime Lucero and Norma Ortiz
Cover photographs by Donnelly Marks
Interior illustration by Teresa Anderko

ISBN 0-439-05278-5

Contents

Introduction

Creating attractive and educational bulletin boards that enrich your classroom can be a difficult and time-consuming task. In *25 Totally Awesome & Totally Easy Bulletin Boards*, I have collected a selection of bulletin boards that I've used successfully in my classroom.

When I create bulletin boards I keep three principles in mind. The bulletin boards should be interactive and make the classroom "come alive" with the curriculum we are studying. They should give my students a sense of ownership of the classroom by surrounding them with examples of their work. Finally, they should be mostly created by students. I like to set the bulletin boards up and let students do the rest.

In this book, you'll find bulletin boards for language arts, math, science, and social studies that you can easily integrate into your classroom. For example, What a Character!, Distinguished Desktops, and A Range of Problems offer interesting ways for students to respond to literature. The Age of Exploration complements a study of explorers and The One-Minute Time Club adds a fun twist to reviewing basic math skills.

I've also included bulletin boards to help you with classroom management. Set up Here's the Scoop, An Apple a Day, and Up, Up and Away in September and you can use them all year to take attendance, manage classroom jobs, and reinforce good behavior.

You'll find step-by-step directions for creating each bulletin board, as well as templates and reproducible student pages to make assembling the bulletin boards a snap!

I hope these bulletin boards brighten and enrich your classroom as they have mine. Enjoy!

The Sky's the Limit!

Welcome a new class with a bulletin
board you create together

Materials

Airplane template (page 6)
Sky Diver template (page 7)
string

Creating the Bulletin Board

♦ Create a sky background
with blue bulletin-board
paper. Cut cloud shapes
from white paper and staple
to the blue background.

♦ Copy the airplane on page
6. Write your name in the
box on the airplane and
color the plane and pilot
with markers or crayons. Glue the plane, wings, and tail fin to a piece of cardboard and cut them
out. This makes them sturdier. You can also laminate the pieces for extra durability.

♦ Using an art knife, cut along the dotted line in the middle of the plane. Insert the airplane wing
into the slit, fold the tab over, and tape it to the back of the plane.

♦ Cut along the dotted line below the tail of the plane. Insert the tail fin into the slit, fold the tab
over, and tape to the back of the plane. Staple the plane to the bulletin board.

♦ Cut white bulletin-board paper into a strip that is approximately 3 feet by 6 inches. Cut a V-
shape on the right end of the banner. Write THE SKY'S THE LIMIT! across the banner.

♦ Tape two pieces of string to the top and bottom of the banner. Staple the banner behind the
plane. Connect the two strings from the banner to the back of the plane, so it looks like the plane
is pulling the banner. For a 3-D effect, curve the paper outward a few times—it will look like it's
blowing in the breeze.

♦ Make a copy of the Sky Diver template for each student in your class. Each student will also
need four pieces of string, each 4-inches long.

♦ Have students follow the directions on the page to assemble their sky divers.

♦ To attach the sky divers to the bulletin board, put a piece of tape behind each of the tabs on the
parachute, so that the sticky side is facing forward.

♦ Bend the tabs back and tape the parachute to the bulletin board. To make the parachute look
three-dimensional, curve the parachute outward. You can either let the sky divers hang freely or
tape their feet to the bulletin board.

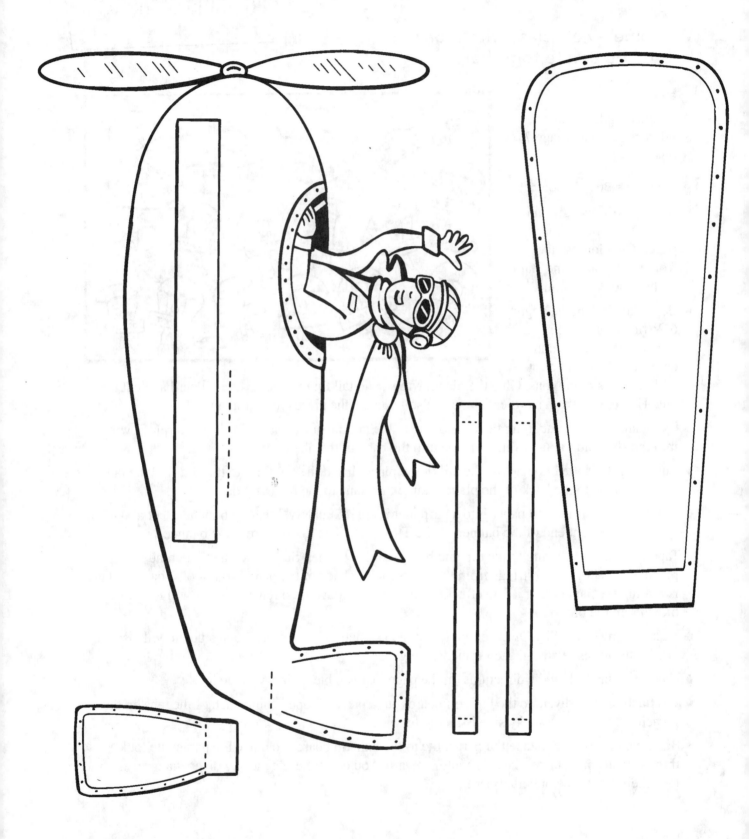

The Sky's the Limit! Sky Diver template

How to Make Your Sky Diver:

1. Write your name on the sign the sky diver is holding.

2. Color in the sky diver and parachute. Then cut out both pieces.

3. Tape a piece of string behind each of the four points of the parachute. Each piece of string should be about 4-inches long.

4. Attach the four pieces of string behind the sky diver's shoulder.

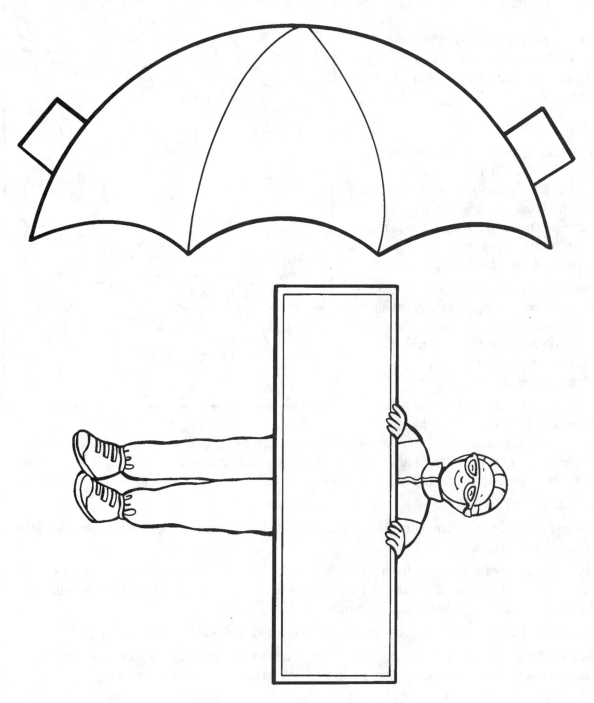

25 Totally Awesome & Totally Easy Bulletin Boards
Scholastic Professional Books

Here's the Scoop

Try this cool way to keep track of class jobs.

Materials

Ice Cream Cone templates (pages 9–10)
a roll of Velcro tape or Velcro dots
one cardboard bucket (from a fast-food chicken restaurant or a craft store.)
white puffy paint (available at craft stores)
sticky tack (available at teaching-supply stores)

Creating the Bulletin Board

♦ Make copies of the Ice Cream Cone templates. You'll need an ice cream cone for each class job and an ice cream scoop for each student. Glue the templates to sheets of cardboard to make them sturdier, then cut out the ice cream cones and ice cream scoops.

♦ Color the ice cream cones brown and the ice cream scoops a variety of colors. Using a thick marker, write a student's name on each ice cream scoop. Use puffy paint to write the names of the class jobs on the cones.

♦ Cut the cardboard bucket in half vertically. Cover one of the halves with construction paper. Be sure to cover the open side of the bucket with construction paper. Write ICE CREAM on the front of the bucket. Staple the bucket to the center of the bulletin board, with the rounded side facing out. (See the illustration above.)

♦ Use sticky tack to affix the ice cream cones around the bucket.

♦ Put a small piece of Velcro on the back of each ice cream scoop and attach the other side of the Velcro above each ice cream cone.

♦ As you select a student for each class job, stick his or her ice cream scoop above the ice cream cone. That student will be in charge of that job for the week. After you have selected students for each job, put any remaining ice cream scoops in the bucket.

♦ If a class job requires two or three students, give the cone a double or triple scoop.

♦ At the start of each week, rotate the jobs among the students. To keep track of what job each student has performed, make a notation on the back of his or her ice cream scoop.

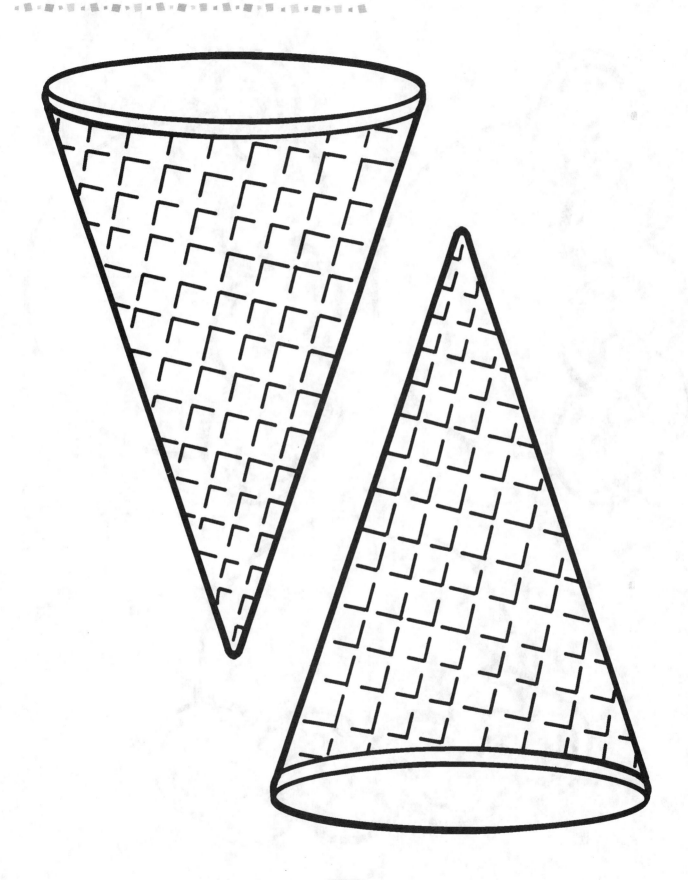

25 Totally Awesome & Totally Easy Bulletin Boards
Scholastic Professional Books

An Apple a Day

Create this bulletin board for a quick-and-easy way to take attendance.

Materials

Apple template (page 12)
a roll of Velcro tape

Creating the Bulletin Board

♦ You can create this bulletin board before the start of school or have the students help you make it as a first-day activity. Use a bulletin board near the door so that it is convenient when students walk into the classroom in the morning.

♦ Start by creating a large apple tree and two large baskets. You can draw the tree and baskets or construct them out of colored bulletin board paper. Place the title AN APPLE A DAY… at the top of the display.

♦ Create title strips for each of the baskets. I use GOING HOME FOR LUNCH and EATING LUNCH AT SCHOOL. You can create different titles depending on the lunch choices your students need to make, such as BAG LUNCH and CAFETERIA LUNCH.

♦ Place two long horizontal strips of Velcro tape over each basket, so that the tape looks like bands around the baskets.

♦ Make copies of the Apple template on page 12. You will need one apple for each student. Glue the template to a sheet of cardboard to make it sturdy. Color the apples and write a student's name on each apple. Then cut the apples out. (For extra durability, laminate the apples.)

♦ Place a small piece of Velcro tape on the back of each apple and the matching piece of Velcro in the tree.

Using the Bulletin Board

♦ Each morning the apples should be on the tree. As students arrive they should take their apples and place them on the appropriate basket. The apples on the tree reflect absent students. The names on the baskets make it easy for you to take a lunch count quickly.

♦ When the students return from lunch they should put their apples back on the tree so the bulletin board is ready for the next day. Any apples that remain in the baskets reflect students who did not return from lunch.

Up, Up, and Away!

Encourage good behavior with a bulletin board that helps the whole class work toward a goal.

Materials

Hot Air Balloon template (page 14)
string

Creating the Bulletin Board

♦ Create a sky background with blue bulletin board paper. Cut 25 clouds out of white construction paper and arrange them in an *S* formation from the bottom of the board to the top. On the last cloud, write "Goal." Add a long cloud-shaped banner at the top of the bulletin board that reads UP, UP, AND AWAY!

♦ Color the Hot Air Balloon template and then cut both pieces out. You can laminate the pieces so they will last all year.

♦ Assemble the balloon by taping four pieces of string behind the balloon. Then attach the strings behind the basket of the hot air balloon.

♦ Fold the tabs on the hot air balloon backward and tack them above the bottom-left cloud on the bulletin board. Curve the balloon outward so it looks three-dimensional. Let the basket hang freely.

Using the Bulletin Board

♦ Whenever the entire class is on task, is behaving exceptionally well, or has participated quietly in a fire drill, move the balloon one cloud closer to the goal. You usually don't even have to announce the move; someone will see you move it and word will spread quickly. You can also move the balloon in the other direction if the entire class is still off task after a verbal warning. This will help them return to their work quickly. When the class reaches the goal, reward them with a special privilege or treat, such as a popcorn party, an extra hour of outside activities, or a favorite video.

Option

♦ You can also use this bulletin board to track the class progress toward a goal. For example, the entire class attempting to read 100 books or collect 100 cans for a food drive. You can add more clouds to the display or have the cloud represent increments of five.

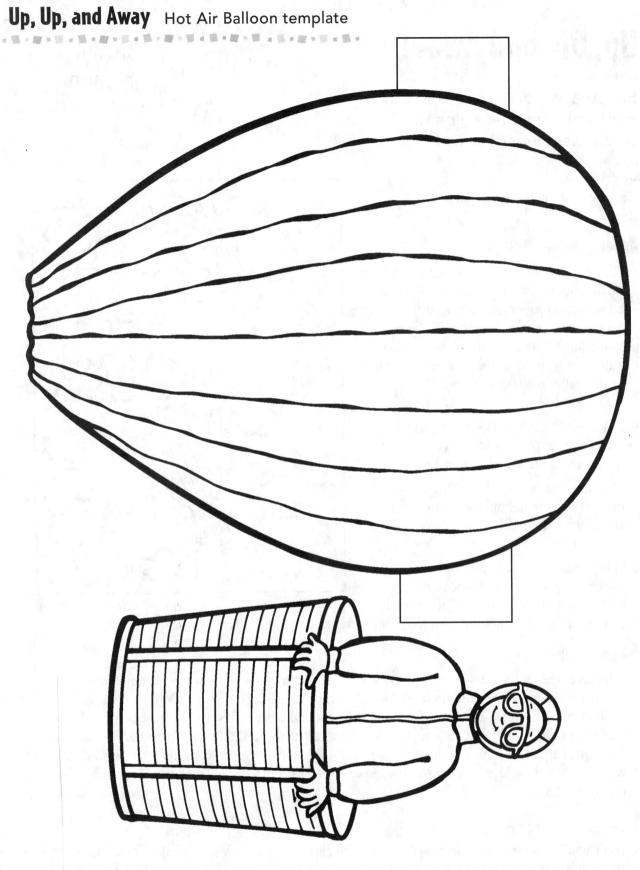

25 Totally Awesome & Totally Easy Bulletin Boards
Scholastic Professional Books

Distinguished Desktops

Students display what they know about a famous person's life by designing that person's desktop.

Materials

Biography Graphic Organizer (page 16)   large sheets of brown construction paper

Setting Up

♦ Cover your bulletin board with any color bulletin-board paper and add a banner that reads DISTINGUISHED DESKTOPS. To make the banner look like a scroll, curl the two edges in.

Creating the Bulletin Board

♦ After students each read a biography of a famous person, have them report on what they've learned by creating a desk blotter that represents each person's life. Student can use the Biography Graphic Organizer to record key facts about the person.

♦ Give each student a large sheet of brown construction paper. They should decorate it so that it looks like a desk blotter. Then have students add the following elements to their desktop:

1. A sign that reads FROM THE DESK OF (Name of Famous Person).

2. A letter from the famous person. Students should design a piece of stationery that reflects the person they researched and use the stationery to write a letter from that person's point of view. The letter should include information about the "writer" and should explain who the letter's recipient is and why he or she was important to the famous person.

3. Three items that represent the person. For explain, Amelia Earhart's desktop might include a map with her route drawn on it, a model airplane, and a compass. Students should try to make the items as three-dimensional as possible.

4. Three short notes that the person might have written to himself or herself. Students can write the notes on stick-on note paper and attach them to the desktop.

♦ Once students have completed their desktops, they should give short presentations about their subject and the significance of the objects on the desktop.

♦ Hang the desktops on the bulletin board.

Name _____

Use this graphic organizer to help you research your biography subject.

BIRTH

When:

Where:

DEATH

When:

Where:

NATIONALITY

EDUCATION

Dates, Schools, Degrees:

EXPERIENCES

Experiences that helped mold this person:

MARRIAGES

Dates and names of spouses:

CHILDREN/FAMILY LIFE

IMPORTANT PEOPLE

Names of important people and their significance to this person:

PROBLEMS

What were some problems this person had to overcome?

NAME OF PERSON

ACCOMPLISHMENTS

Major accomplishments and contributions:

INTERESTING FACTS

25 Totally Awesome & Totally Easy Bulletin Boards
Scholastic Professional Books

An In-depth Look at Books

Plot the key points of any book you read in class with a three-dimensional display.

Materials

craft materials (cotton, yarn, buttons, cardboard, craft sticks, etc.)
shirt boxes (you'll need half a box for each chapter)
large index cards

Setting Up

♦ Cover your bulletin board with any color bulletin board paper and add a banner that reads AN IN-DEPTH LOOK AT (title of book).

Creating the Bulletin Board

♦ Assembling this bulletin board is a wonderful culminating activity for any novel you have read together in class. After you've finished reading, divide the class into as many groups as there are chapters in the book.

♦ Assign each group a chapter and ask them to reread it and discuss the main idea in the chapter.

♦ Next, each group should construct a shadow box that features the characters acting out the main event from that chapter. Each group should use half a shirt box to stage the scene and use construction paper and other craft materials to create the interior. For a more finished look, groups can wrap the outside of the shirt boxes in construction paper.

♦ Each group should also write a summary of the chapter and a description of the event on a large index card. They can hang the card from the bottom of the box.

♦ Hang the shadow boxes in chronological order across the bulletin board.

Language Arts

What a Character!

Students exhibit their understanding of main characters with fun-to-make character figures.

Materials

large index cards   Character template (page 19)   oaktag

Setting Up

♦ Cover the bulletin board with any color paper and add a banner that reads WHAT A CHARACTER!

Creating the Bulletin Board

♦ After students have completed reading a novel—either one you have read in class or one they have read independently—have them do a character study of any of the main characters using the Character template.

♦ Give each student a copy of the Character template (page 19). Following the directions on the template, students should draw the character, glue the template to a sheet of oaktag and cut it out. Then they should draw or construct three items (or props) that reflect the unique qualities of the character and then cut them out. For example, if a student was creating a character study of *Maniac Magee*, they might add a package of butterscotch Krimpets, a baseball glove, and their interpretation of Cobble's Knot.

♦ On a large index card, have students write the title of the book and the character's name across the top. Underneath the title, they should write a paragraph describing the character's personality, interesting qualities, what the props signify, and what role the character plays in the story. Students should use a thesaurus to find uncommon adjectives to describe the character (not words such as *nice*, *happy*, or *pretty*). Students should write their names on the bottom of the index card.

♦ Staple the characters with their props and the accompanying descriptions to the bulletin board.

What a Character! Character template

How to Make Your Character Template:

1. Draw your character on the template below. Try to match your picture to the description of the character in the book.

2. Glue the template to a sheet of oaktag, then cut the figure out.

3. Create three props for the character. The props should reflect the unique qualities of the character.

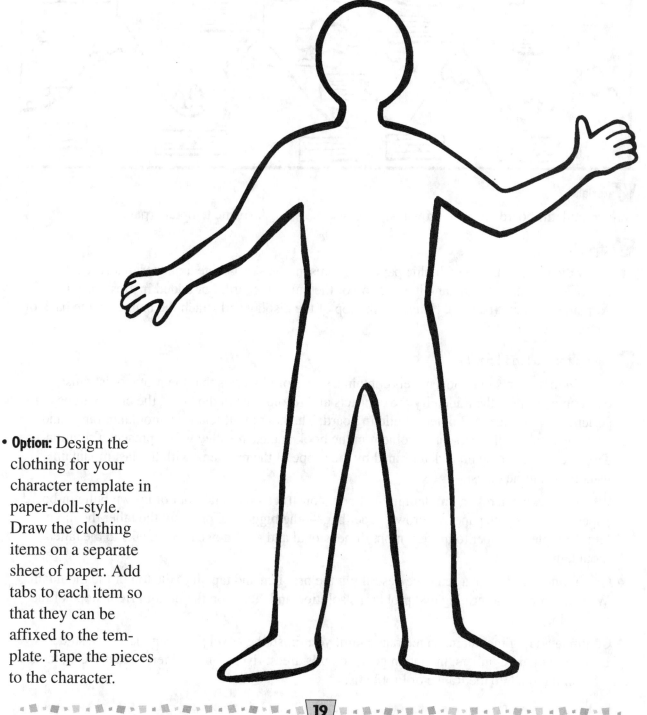

• **Option:** Design the clothing for your character template in paper-doll-style. Draw the clothing items on a separate sheet of paper. Add tabs to each item so that they can be affixed to the template. Tape the pieces to the character.

A Range of Problems

Chart the obstacles a protagonist faces with a bulletin board that illustrates the conflicts and resolutions in a book.

Materials

brown bulletin-board paper or brown paper bags   Airplane template (page 6)

Setting Up

♦ Cover the bulletin board with blue paper to represent the sky. Create a banner that reads A RANGE OF PROBLEMS and hang it at the top of the bulletin board. For added interest, use the Airplane template (page 6). Hang it at the top of the display and attach the banner to the back of the plane with the title.

Creating the Bulletin Board

♦ Explain to students that most novels contain a series of obstacles that the protagonist must overcome. To help them identify the conflicts and resolutions in the book, the class will be constructing a A Range of Problems bulletin board. The board will feature a mountain range and each mountain will represent a problem in the book and each valley will represent a solution. The size of the mountain is determined by the scope of the problem, with the last mountain usually being the tallest.

♦ When you come across a problem in the book, construct a mountain out of brown bulletin-board paper, butcher block paper, or brown paper bags—the bigger the problem the taller the mountain. Rumple the paper to make it more dimensional and add snowcapped peaks to the taller mountains.

♦ On an index card write a sentence describing the problem and tape it at the top of the mountain. Write a sentence describing that problem's solution and tape it on the bottom right slope of the mountain.

♦ Continue adding mountains to the range until you finish the novel. You can then have students create mountain climbers, mountain goats, clouds, trees, rivers, birds, skiers, chalets, etc., to add a finishing touch to the Range of Problems.

Armfuls of Good Grammar

Here's a whimsical way for students to review the eight parts of speech.

Materials

Octopus template (page 22)
Treasure Chest templates (page 23)
blue bulletin board paper

Setting Up

♦ Cover the bulletin board with blue paper to create an ocean background. Copy and cut out the Octopus template. Color the octopus in and then create arms by cutting out strips of the same color bulletin-board paper. To make the arms appear three-dimensional, accordion-fold them. Staple the head and the arms to the bulletin board. Add a banner that reads ARMFULS OF GOOD GRAMMAR.

♦ Make copies of the Treasure Chest templates (page 23). On each treasure chest, write the name of one of the parts of speech. Staple a treasure chest near each of the octopus's arms.

♦ **Option**: To create a larger octopus, copy the template on an overhead transparency and project a larger version of the octopus on a sheet of bulletin board paper; trace.

Creating the Bulletin Board

♦ Review the parts of speech with the class. Then as a class, brainstorm examples of each part of speech. In keeping with the ocean theme of the bulletin board, ask students to think of words related to the sea. Use the following prompts to encourage students:

Nouns: People, places, and things associated with the sea (sailor, Black Sea, starfish)

Verbs: Things you can do in the sea (swim, sail, dive)

Adjectives: Words that describe the sea (rough, blue, deep)

Adverbs: Sea-related phrases containing adverbs (*swiftly* flowing, *very* strong current)

Pronouns: Sea-related phrases containing pronouns (*his* snorkel, *their* sharp teeth)

Prepositions: Prepositional phrases about the sea (*on* the beach, *under* the surface)

Interjections: Sea-related sentences which begin with an interjection (*Hey*, look what I found!)

Conjunctions: Conjunctions that join two similar words related to the sea (saltwater *and* freshwater, crabs *and* shrimp)

♦ As you gather students' suggestions, write the words and phrases on strips of white paper or self-sticking note paper and post them near the appropriate treasure chest.

♦ An alternative way to complete this bulletin board is to have students work in small groups to come up with examples of one part of speech or one example of each part of speech.

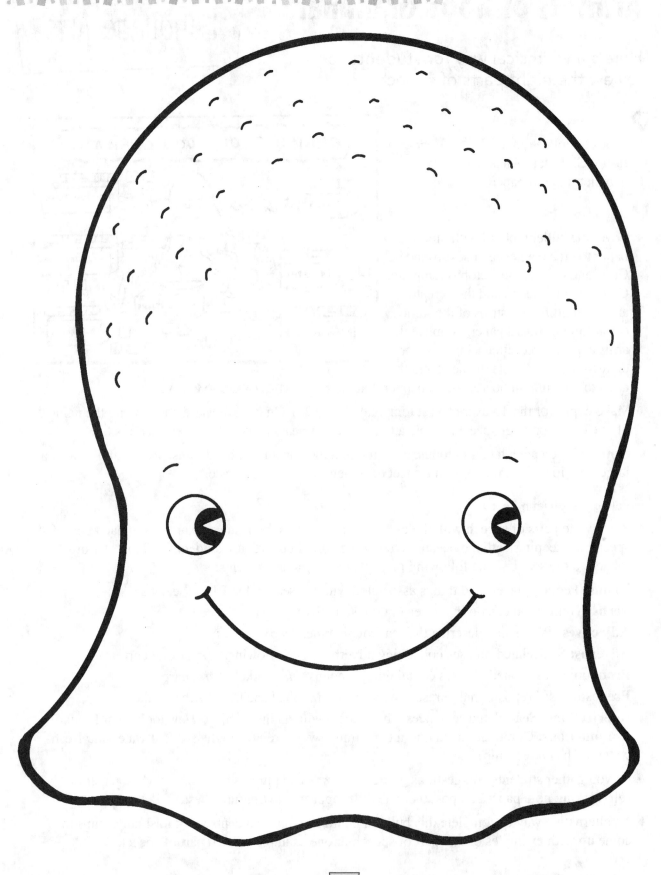

25 Totally Awesome & Totally Easy Bulletin Boards
Scholastic Professional Books

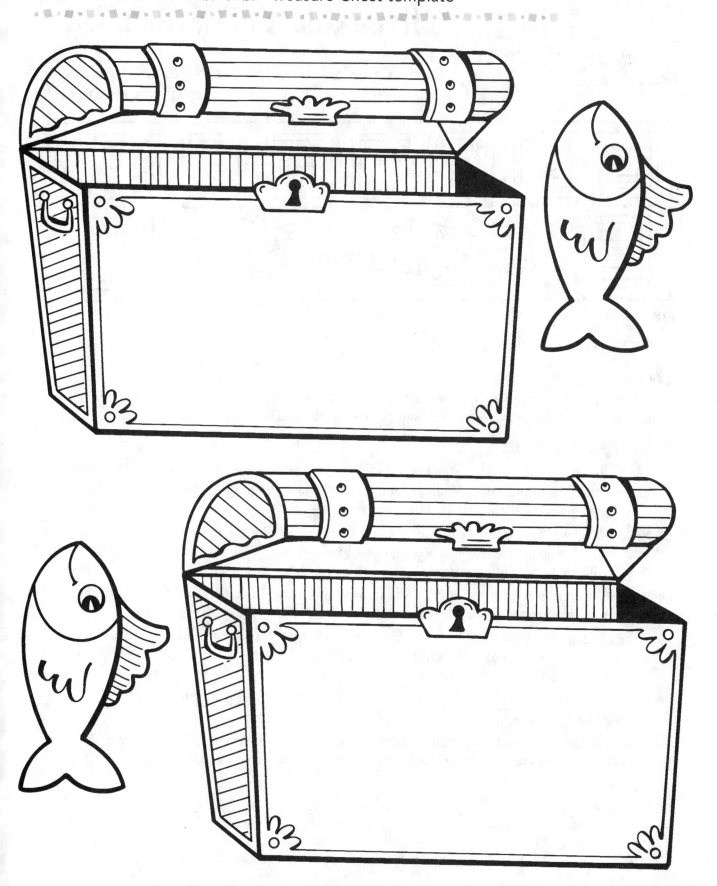

Language Arts

All the Colors of the Rainbow

Design a colorful display that features students' poems about the colors of the rainbow.

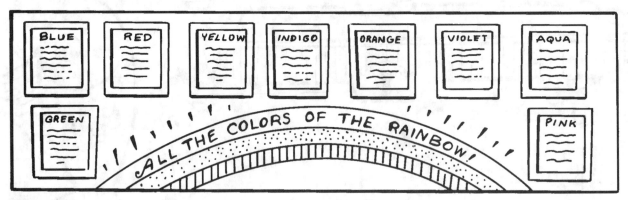

Materials

construction paper in assorted colors

Setting Up

♦ Cover the bulletin board with white paper. Add a rainbow-shaped banner that reads ALL THE COLORS OF THE RAINBOW. Write each letter of the title in a different color.

Creating the Bulletin Board

♦ Begin by asking students to each pick a color and then brainstorm and list all of the objects that make them think of that color. Students should include not only things that *are* that color, but things that they think "taste, smell, sound, and feel" like that color.

♦ Next, challenge students to take this list and use it to write a poem about the color. To get students started, read them the poems below. You might also share Charlotte Zolotow's poem "Red" with students to inspire them.

♦ Remind students that their poems can feature rhyming words, alliteration, and assonance. They also can use metaphors, similes, and personification to describe objects.

♦ Once students have completed their poems, they should write their final version in the center of a sheet of white paper. The poem's title should be the color. Then students can create a border made up of objects mentioned in the poem.

♦ Finally, have students frame their poems in the color by gluing their poems to a sheet of matching construction paper.

♦ Post all of the poems on the bulletin board. Work with students to arrange the poems in a pleasing manner, either grouping colors together or scattering them in an interesting pattern.

WHITE
White is the color of an Arctic fox
It's the lightest color in a crayon box.
It represents good in Old West flix
It's the color of a bundle of aspen sticks.

YELLOW
Yellow is the color a coward feels.
Yellow is the flavor of banana peels.
It falls from the sky on a bright summer's day.
It's the center of daisies, and the scent of hay.

In Other Words...

Rid students' writing of tired, over-used words with a game that becomes a bulletin-board display.

Materials

white bulletin board paper

Setting Up

♦ Cover the bulletin board with light colored paper, then staple another large sheet of the same color bulletin-board paper over the background. (Students will be writing on the top sheet.) Create a banner that reads IN OTHER WORDS . . .

Creating the Bulletin Board

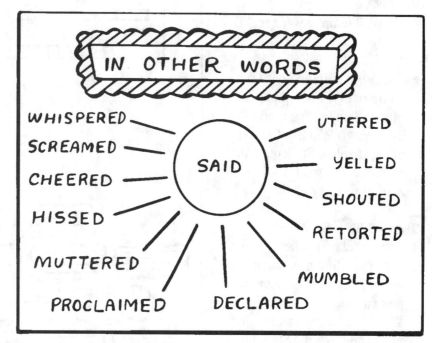

♦ You may notice that there are some words that tend to show up in students' writing over and over again. This activity will inspire students to think more creatively about their word choices and introduce them to new word options.

♦ Draw a large circle in the middle of the bulletin board with a black marker and write a commonly used word in it (for example, *said*).

♦ Randomly select students to go to the board and draw a line from the center circle and write another way the word can be conveyed (such as *uttered, whispered, shouted*). They should print the words in large, dark letters.

♦ Continue selecting students to add words to the board. If a student cannot think of another word, he is eliminated from play. Continue playing until there is only one student left.

♦ Leave this chart up for one or two weeks. Each day during the first minute of language class invite students to add new words to the list.

♦ Repeat this activity every week or two. After a while students naturally learn to expand their word choices to make their writing more descriptive and lively.

Words to Use				
walk	said	ate	big	asked
happy	sad	nice	pretty	like
saw	small	think	home	fast

Language Arts

The Word Wall

Build a word wall to help students learn and review vocabulary and spelling words.

Materials

Word Wall templates (page 27)

Setting Up

♦ Cover the bulletin board with white bulletin-board paper. Place a banner that reads THE WORD WALL at the top of the display. Students will construct the word wall by adding word bricks.

Creating the Bulletin Board

♦ As your class studies a new list of spelling or vocabulary words, have each student complete a word study, using the Word Wall template, for one of the new words. Students can complete this in class or as a homework assignment.

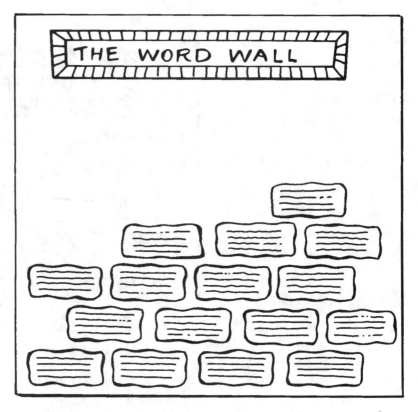

♦ Review each of the following items on the template so that students understand how to complete the word study:

1. The Spelling/Vocabulary Word: Students write the word across the top of the template in large letters. Students write the part of speech next to the word.

2. Number of Syllables: Students break the word into syllables (i.e., syl • la • bles).

3. Icon: Students draw an icon that conveys the meaning of the word. The icon can be a simple symbol in the style of a road sign or map. They will have to be creative if the word is not a noun.

4. Sentence: Students use the word in a sentence that demonstrates the meaning of the word.

♦ Once students have completed their word studies, have them review their findings with the class so that everyone has a greater understanding of the new words.

♦ Next, have students hang the word studies on the bulletin board to form bricks for your Word Wall. Another option is to copy the template onto red or tan paper to create colored bricks.

Word: _____   Syllables: _____

Synonym: _____   Antonym: _____

Sentence: _____   Icon:

_____

_____

_____

Word: _____   Syllables: _____

Synonym: _____   Antonym: _____

Sentence: _____   Icon:

_____

_____

_____

Word: _____   Syllables: _____

Synonym: _____   Antonym: _____

Sentence: _____   Icon:

_____

_____

_____

In the News

Keep students up to date on current events by posting articles from the newspaper on your "In the News" board.

Materials

color comics from the Sunday newspaper
Article Summary reproducible (page 30)

Days of the Week template (page 29)

Setting Up

♦ Cover a small bulletin board, or a section of a bulletin board, with the comics from the Sunday newspaper. (You'll need a space approximately 3 by 2 feet for this display.) Copy the Days of the Week template and cut out each of the titles. Center the title IN THE NEWS at the top of the bulletin board. Add the names of the days of the week under the main title.

Creating the Bulletin Board

♦ Explain to the class that each day a different student will be responsible for finding an interesting article in the newspaper and reporting on it to the class. Then the article will be posted on the In the News board for everyone to read.

♦ Before students present their articles to the class, remind them to speak loudly and clearly and to maintain eye contact with the class. To help students remember the important points of the article as they discuss it with the class, have them complete the Article Summary on page 30.

♦ After the oral presentation, open the floor up to questions from the class. After the discussion ends, staple the article to the bulletin board under the appropriate day of the week, replacing last week's article. Keep articles posted for a full week so that the entire class will have an opportunity to read the story. You can also post students' article summaries.

About Public Speaking

Public speaking is an important skill that should be nurtured at all grade levels. The more a person speaks in front of a group, the more comfortable he or she will become, and the more his or her self-confidence will increase. This ongoing bulletin board is a wonderful way to foster this skill. It is also a great vehicle for generating class discussions about what is happening in the world around you.

Monday

Tuesday

Wednesday

Thursday

Friday

In The News

25 Totally Awesome & Totally Easy Bulletin Boards
Scholastic Professional Books

Name: _____ Presentation Date: _____

When discussing your news article, be sure to include the following points:

Article Headline: _____

Name of Newspaper: _____

Who is the article about?: _____

What is the article about?: _____

Where does it take place?: _____

When does it take place?: _____

Why did you choose this article? (Do not say, "Because it was interesting."):

_____

_____

Name: _____ Presentation Date: _____

When discussing your news article, be sure to include the following points:

Article Headline: _____

Name of Newspaper: _____

Who is the article about?: _____

What is the article about?: _____

Where does it take place?: _____

When does it take place?: _____

Why did you choose this article? (Do not say, "Because it was interesting."):

_____

_____

25 Totally Awesome & Totally Easy Bulletin Boards
Scholastic Professional Books

The Nifty Fifty-First

Students apply what they know about geography, states, and more when they invent a fifty-first state.

Materials

Travel Brochure templates (pages 32 and 33)

Setting Up

♦ Cover the bulletin board with any color paper. Add a banner that reads THE NIFTY FIFTY-FIRST and staple it across the bulletin board. Add a map of the United States in the center of the display.

Creating the Bulletin Board

♦ Explain to the class that they will be using their creativity, as well as their knowledge of geography and the states, to invent a fictitious fifty-first state.

♦ Hand out copies of the Travel Brochure template. Copy pages 32 and 33 back-to-back to make the travel brochure two-sided. Instructions for completing the brochure are on the back panel.

♦ Tell students to name the state after their first or last names just like certain states were named after people (Georgia, Maryland, New York, Louisiana). They should try to come up with creative names like "Mattlantis," or "Joansboro."

♦ Review statistics for several states—state bird, state song, state flower, state motto, etc.—so students have a reference point when selecting or designing ones for their new state.

♦ Students should compose a state song to the melody of a well-known song, such as "Twinkle, Twinkle Little Star." The song should reflect aspects of the state's topography, attractions, weather, or natural resources.

♦ On a separate sheet of white construction paper, students should draw a map of their state. Depending on their own interests, they can create a state that has islands, mountains, beaches, forests, rivers, deserts, waterfalls, or lakes. It can be hot, cold, snowy, rainy, or dry. They should include a map key.

♦ Hang the maps and brochures on the bulletin board. Staple the back panel of the brochure to the bulletin board and allow the top two panels to open freely.

Option: The Nifty Fifty

You can also use this travel brochure format for a study of the United States. Students can complete the brochures using real information for the 50 states.

DIRECTIONS

Fold page in thirds, so that the edge of panel 5 meets the line that separates panels 3 and 4. Fold panel 3 to the right so that its left edge meets the right edge of panel 2.

Completing Your Travel Brochure

COVER: Include the name of your state, your name, and an illustration a popular tourist attraction in your state.

PANEL 2: Draw one picture of a natural feature and one picture of a man-made attraction. Write a complete, detailed sentence describing each picture.

PANEL 3: *Top:* List the top-ten reasons people would visit your state. List natural and man-made attractions, sports, festivals, and more. *Bottom:* Write a descriptive paragraph about the state's topography, weather patterns, and temperature.

PANEL 4: Draw a picture of your state flag, the state bird, and the state flower. Write the name of the bird and the flower on the line under the picture.

PANEL 5: *Top:* Write the lyrics to your state song. Base them on aspects of your state—weather, landforms, attractions, etc. Set them to the tune of a well-known song. *Bottom:* Write a few sentences describing the major economic resources that generate revenue for your state

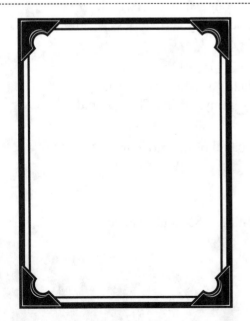

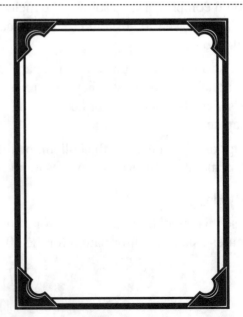

State Song

_____

_____

_____

_____

_____

_____

_____

_____

Sung to the tune of: _____

State Economy

_____

_____

_____

_____

State Flag

[ ]

State Bird

[ ]

State Flower

[ ]

_____

The Top 10 Reasons to Visit Our State

1. _____
2. _____
3. _____
4. _____
5. _____
6. _____
7. _____
8. _____
9. _____
10. _____

About Our State

_____

_____

_____

_____

From Sea to Shining Sea

Students design informational posters about the five regions of the United States.

Materials

5 sheets of bulletin-board paper (approximately 3 by 4 feet) in assorted colors
From Sea to Shining Sea requirements reproducible (page 35)
Snapshots template (page 36)
Postcards template (page 37)

Setting Up

♦ Set aside space on a bulletin board for five large posters. Create a banner that reads FROM SEA TO SHINING SEA, and staple it to the bulletin board.

Creating the Bulletin Board

♦ Break the class up into five groups. Explain to the class that each group will research and report on a different region of the United States—Northeast, Southeast, Southwest, West, and Middle West. The groups will present the results of their research in a poster.

♦ Pass out copies of the From Sea to Shining Sea requirements sheet to students and review it with the class. Each group's poster should include all of the elements listed on the requirement sheet. It will be up to each group to decide which member will be responsible for completing each element. I always tell students that part of their final grade will be determined by how well they share in the production of the poster. If someone finishes his or her section of the poster, he or she should help the other members. I also remind students that each member of the group is also responsible for proofreading the *entire* poster.

♦ As students finish each element, they should attach it to the large sheet of bulletin board paper. Each group should use a different color.

♦ Once students have completed their posters, display them under the FROM SEA TO SHINING SEA banner.

From Sea to Shining Sea   Requirement Sheet

TITLE
♦ Write the region you researched across the top of the poster and list the complete name of each group member.

MAP OF THE REGION
♦ On a large sheet of white paper, draw a map of all of the states that are included in your region. Include major landforms such as mountains, deserts, and bodies of water.
♦ Draw a small outline of the United States next to your map. Shade in your region.

CLIMATE
♦ Create a graph that illustrates the average temperature and rainfall in your region during each month of the year.
♦ Underneath the graph, write a paragraph describing what makes the climate in your region unique.
♦ Add the title CLIMATE and attach the graph to your poster.

ECONOMY
♦ Research the top three sources of revenue for your region. Draw three icons that represent these sources. Write a few sentences describing each. Arrange them in an attractive display.
♦ Add the title ECONOMY and attach the page to your poster.

POPULATION
♦ Create a pictograph that illustrates the populations of each the states in your region. Include the total population for the entire region.
♦ Add the title POPULATION and attach the graph to your poster.

NATURAL RESOURCES
♦ Create a chart or graphic organizer that details the natural resources found in your region. It should describe each of the resources and explain how they are beneficial.
♦ Add the title NATURAL RESOURCES and attach the chart to your poster.

MAJOR GEOLOGIC FEATURES
♦ Each group member should choose one interesting geologic feature from the region and research it. Then write a paragraph and draw a detailed picture on the Snapshot template.
♦ Cut Snapshot template out and attach it to a sheet of construction paper. Leave a 1/2 inch border around it. Attach the paragraphs to your poster

MAJOR ATTRACTIONS
♦ Each group member should research one major attraction in the region. It can be anything from a historic site to a popular tourist destination. Use the postcard template to report on the attraction. Glue the template to a sheet of oaktag and then cut out. On one side draw a picture of the attraction. On the other side, write a paragraph about the attraction. Draw a colorful stamp and address the card.
♦ Add the postcards to your poster. Attach only one side of the postcard to the poster so readers can see both the front and back of the card.

35

25 Totally Awesome & Totally Easy Bulletin Boards
Scholastic Professional Books

25 Totally Awesome & Totally Easy Bulletin Boards
Scholastic Professional Books

The Age of Exploration

Sail the seas with the great explorers!

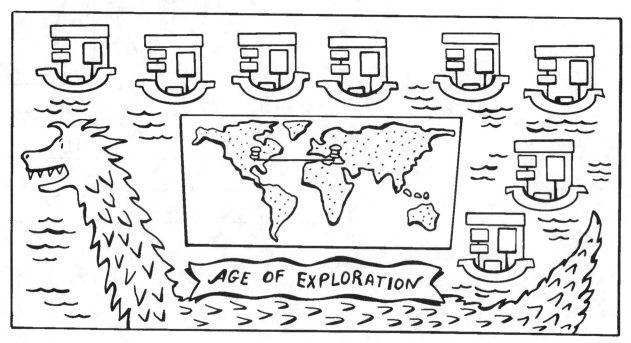

Materials

Ship templates (page 39)
string or yarn

world map
yellow and green construction paper

Setting Up

♦ Cover the bulletin board with blue bulletin-board paper and tack a large world map to the center of the bulletin board.

♦ For a more elaborate display, you can add a sea serpent to the bottom of the bulletin board. To create a sea serpent, draw the outline of one on a large sheet of paper. Have students draw the sea serpent's scales or have them cut the scales from green and yellow construction paper and glue them to the sea sepent's outline. Staple the serpent to the bulletin board. Add wavy, blue corrugated paper around the border for a wavelike effect.

Creating the Bulletin Board

♦ Make a copy of the Ship template for each explorer you will be studying. Glue the templates on to sheets of oaktag to make them more durable. As you study each explorer, pick one student to complete and then color the ship. Another alternative is to have students independently research explorers, complete the templates, and then report their findings to the class.

♦ When students have completed a ship, they should cut it out and tack it to the bulletin board. Then they should use a piece of string to show the route (or routes) the explorer took on the map. Students can match the color of the string to the color of the ship for easy reference. For example, students might color Columbus' ship blue and mark his routes with blue string.

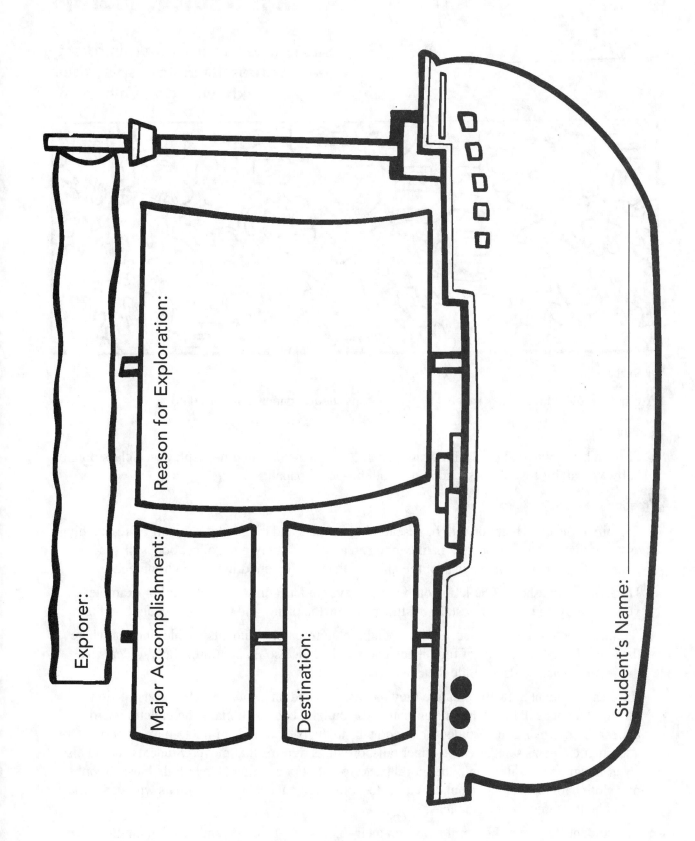

Reason for Exploration:

Explorer:

Major Accomplishment:

Destination:

Student's Name:

Animal Habitat Murals

Students create a mural of a rain forest, ocean, or grasslands to display their knowledge of a habitat.

Materials

Animal Fact Card templates (page 41)   construction paper in assorted colors

Setting Up

♦ Cover a large bulletin board with white paper. You can also create this display on a classroom or hallway wall by covering a section with bulletin-board paper.

Creating the Bulletin Board

♦ Explain to the class that you will be researching animals and their habitats. Start by researching as a class what the environment is like in the area you are studying. Collect books that include photos of the area and make lists of the animals that can be found in that environment.

♦ Then, on a large sheet of bulletin board paper, have students draw the habitat. For example, if you are studying the rain forest, have students draw the plants and trees you would find there.

♦ Next, ask each student to select a different animal to research. Students should find out where the animal lives, what type of food it eats, how it defends itself, and more. Have students use the Animal Fact Cards to guide their research.

♦ Have each student draw the creature they have researched on a sheet of white construction paper. Students will be adding the animal to the bulletin board. To make the bulletin board appear three-dimensional, students can add tabs to the back of the animal to make it pop out, or add other elements such as crepe-paper tails, or wings or arms that move. Students should also try to integrate the animal into the mural background. For example, they might have a monkey or a sloth hanging from a tree and an anteater foraging on the ground. Animals with camouflage could be the same color as the leaves.

♦ Ask students to give a short oral report on their findings to the class, and attach their creatures and fact cards to the mural.

ANIMAL: _____

Distinguishing Characteristics: _____

Where does it live? _____

What are its social habits? _____

Is it solitary or found in groups? _____

What does it eat? _____

Who are its predators? _____

How does it defend or protect itself? _____

How does it care for its young? _____

Other interesting facts: _____

_____

_____

ANIMAL: _____

Distinguishing Characteristics: _____

Where does it live? _____

What are its social habits? _____

Is it solitary or found in groups? _____

What does it eat? _____

Who are its predators? _____

How does it defend or protect itself? _____

How does it care for its young? _____

Other interesting facts: _____

_____

_____

25 Totally Awesome & Totally Easy Bulletin Boards
Scholastic Professional Books

Science

Look What's Growing!

Plant a garden of flowers to exhibit your students' knowledge of plants.

Materials

Flower templates (pages 43 and 44)

Setting Up

♦ Cover the bulletin board with brown paper so that it looks like a flower bed. Attach a banner that reads LOOK WHAT'S GROWING IN… (your class name here)! and staple it to the bulletin board.

Creating the Bulletin Board

♦ To begin, have students create circle books about plants using the templates on pages 43 and 44. Some suggestions for plant circle books:

Parts of a Flower: Students diagram and label the parts of a flower (petal, ovary, anther, stamen, stem, sepal, pistil, leaf, sepal) and write definitions for each of the plant parts.

Seeds: Students write and illustrate a book about seeds that can include the way seeds are spread, the different types of seeds, where seeds are found in different types of plants, and more.

Concept Books: Students write and illustrate a book about an important concept, such as photosynthesis.

Neighborhood Flora: Students record, with pictures and captions, the different types of plants in the neighborhood.

Experiment Journal: Students keep track of any plant experiments in the circle book, including experiment preparation, results, and more.

♦ After completing the circle book blossoms, students should create a stem and leaves with green construction paper. Staple the stems and leaves to the bulletin board. Then staple the circle book blossoms to the top of the stems.

Look What's Growing Flower template

How to assemble and display the circle book:

1. After cutting out the flowers, fold each one in half.

2. Use a gluestick to attach side 1 to side 2. Then attach side 2 to side 3, etc.

3. Staple the first and last pages directly to the bulletin board. Longer books should first be glued to a sheet of oaktag to make them more durable.

25 Totally Awesome & Totally Easy Bulletin Boards
Scholastic Professional Books

Look What's Growing Flower template 2

Cut this page out along the solid lines. Use this circle book page for writing.

25 Totally Awesome & Totally Easy Bulletin Boards
Scholastic Professional Books

From Asteroids to Zero Gravity

Set up an information center about the solar system with lift-the-flap knowledge charts.

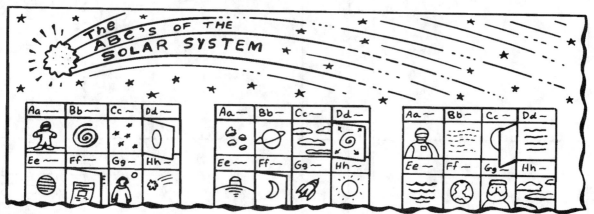

Materials

Lift-the-Flap Knowledge Chart template (page 46)   white bulletin-board paper

Setting Up

♦ Cover the bulletin board with dark blue or black paper. Have students cut small stars out of white paper and scatter them across the background. Create a banner in the shape of a comet that reads THE ABCs OF THE SOLAR SYSTEM.

Creating the Bulletin Board

♦ Lift-the-Flap Knowledge Charts are a terrific tool to help students review all the information they have learned during a unit and they make a fun, interactive information center. To begin, have students brainstorm a list of all the things they learned during your unit on the solar system. Challenge students to find an object for each letter of the alphabet. They can use textbooks, encyclopedias, and other reference materials to complete their lists. Students should also write a brief definition or description of each of the items on their list.

♦ Hand out copies of the Knowledge Chart template and large sheets of white bulletin paper. Each student will need 3 copies of the template and a sheet of paper approximately 12 inches by 20 inches.

♦ In the shaded strip at the top of the template, students should write—in alphabetical order—a letter of the alphabet (in upper and lower case) and the corresponding word from their list. In the box, they should draw a picture that represents the word. Students can combine *W* and *X* and *Y* and *Z*.

♦ Next, have students cut out each panel and create four flaps by cutting the three dotted lines in the middle of the panel up to the shaded strip. Students should arrange the panels in alphabetical order on the large sheet of paper and then glue the shaded strip to the page. Students should write the definition or description that corresponds to each item underneath each flap.

♦ Hang the completed Knowledge Charts on the bulletin board. Students can review what they have learned with a trip to the bulletin board.

From Asteroids to Zero Gravity   Knowledge Chart template

How to Assemble the Knowledge Charts:

1. Following the dotted lines, cut out each panel. Create four flaps by cutting three dotted lines in center up to the shaded box.

2. Use a glue stick to glue the top strip to a large sheet of paper, leaving the bottom of the panels free.

25 Totally Awesome & Totally Easy Bulletin Boards
Scholastic Professional Books

It's Elementary, My Dear

Students assemble interactive data disks that demonstrate the scientific method.

Materials

Data Disk templates
(pages 48 and 49)
brass fasteners

Setting Up

♦ Cover the bulletin board with any color paper and add a banner with the title IT'S ELEMENTARY, MY DEAR to the top of the board

Creating the Bulletin Board

♦ Explain to students that they will be creating data disks that define and demonstrate the five steps of the scientific method. Review with students the steps below:

Step 1: Purpose—What do I want to learn?
Step 2: Hypothesis—What do I think will happen?
Step 3: Experiment—What test will confirm or disprove my hypothesis?
Step 4: Results—What happened during the experiment?
Step 5: Conclusion—What did I learn? Was the hypothesis correct?

There are other elements to conducting a scientific investigation such as doing the research, gathering the materials, and detailing the procedure, but the five steps listed above form the core of the scientific method.

♦ Next ask students to apply the scientific method by devising and carrying out a simple experiment to test a hypothesis. Alternately, students might apply the five steps to an experiment the class has done. (If students will be doing experiments, you might have them work in small groups.)

♦ Once students have completed their experiments, pass out copies of the templates on pages 48 and 49. Students can follow the directions on the template to construct the data disks.

♦ On the cover of the data disk they should write the title of the experiment in creative lettering, draw a related picture, and write their names. On the inside of the data disk, they should outline how their experiment demonstrated the five steps of the scientific method.

♦ After the students have completed their data disks, hang them on the bulletin board. Students will enjoy learning about different experiments by turning the disks

To assemble the data disks:

1. Glue both data disks to a sheet of construction paper or poster board. Cut out each template.

2. Cut out the viewing window on disk 1.

3. Place disk 1 on top of disk 2. Fasten the disks together by pushing a brass fastener through the black dot in the center of disk 1.

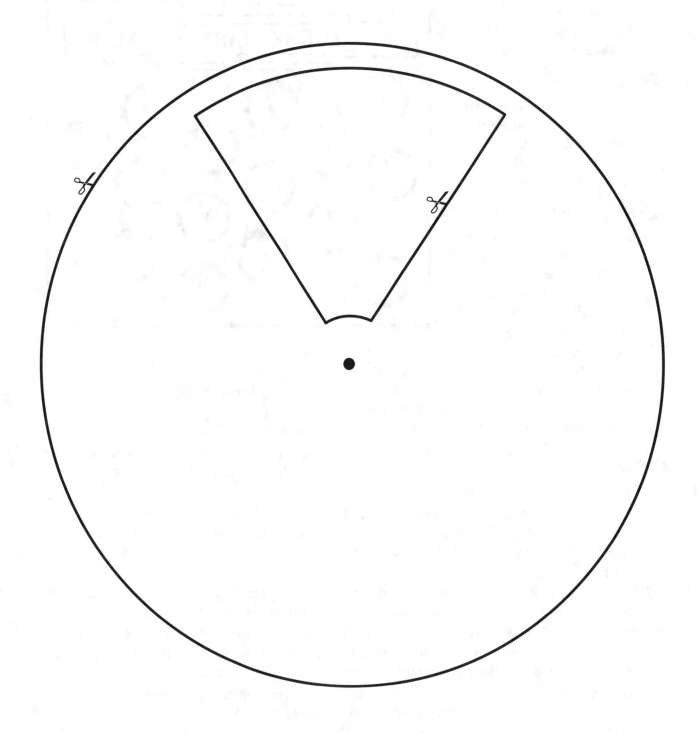

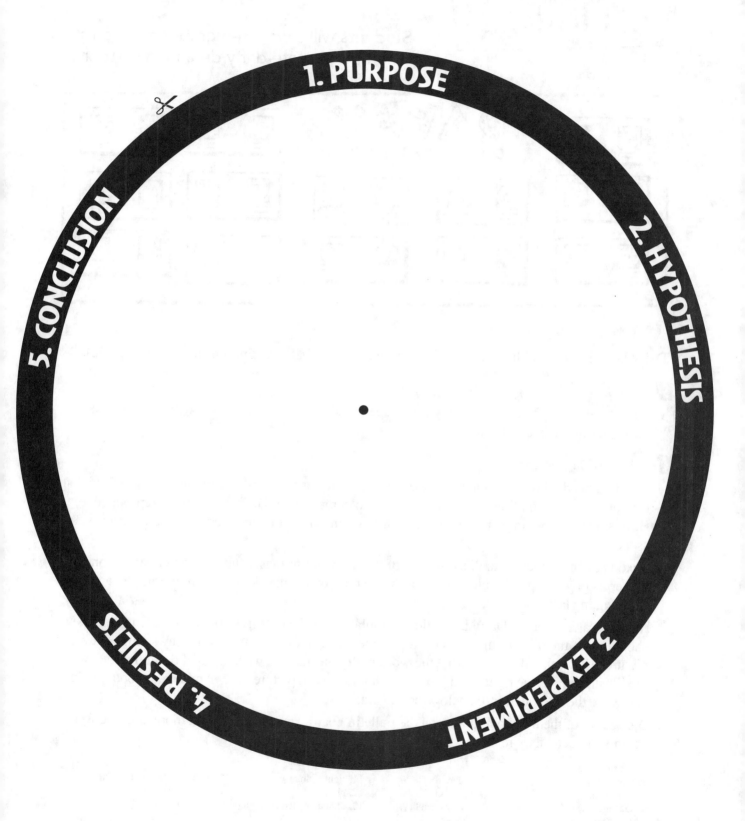

25 Totally Awesome & Totally Easy Bulletin Boards
Scholastic Professional Books

Daffy Definitions

Students will always remember math terms when they create daffy definition cartoons.

Materials

Daffy Definitions Fun Sheet reproducible (page 51)   Daffy Definitions template (page 52)

Setting Up

♦ Cover the bulletin board with any type of paper. Add a banner that reads DAFFY DEFINITIONS to the center of the bulletin board.

Creating the Bulletin Board

♦ Tell students that to help them remember new math terms they will be creating daffy definitions. Introduce daffy definitions by asking students to complete the Daffy Definitions reproducible. Have students work in pairs to match the daffy definition to the math term. Review the answers as a class.

♦ Next, challenge students to illustrate one of the daffy definitions. Students can either use one of the terms on the reproducible or they can write their own daffy definition of a term you are studying in class.

♦ Hand out a copy of the Daffy Definitions template to each student. Explain to students that they should write the math term across the top of the page. In the left-hand box, they should draw a picture or icon that illustrates what the word really means, and write the real definition below the illustration. In the right-hand box, they should draw a picture of the "misunderstood" word, and write the daffy definition below the illustration.

♦ Display all of the daffy definitions on the bulletin board. Have students add more as you cover new math vocabulary in class.

Answers to Fun Sheet:

1. geometry (gee, I'm a tree)
2. word problems
3. circle (Sir Kull)
4. polygon (Polly gone)
5. place value
6. square roots
7. yardstick
8. center (sent her)
9. tangent
10. subtraction
11. right triangle
12. pi
13. diameter (dye amateur)
14. ruler
15. ellipse (eel lips)
16. addition (a dish in)
17. protractors
18. inverse

Name _____

Daffy Definitions Fun Sheet

Dimwit Daffy was asked to define the following math terms. He obviously had trouble deciphering their meanings. Can you match each of the words to Daffy's definitions? Write the word on the line next to the mixed-up meaning. Each word will be used only once.

MATH TERMS

center	word problems	tangent	right triangle
diameter	addition	polygon	protractors
circle	inverse	yardstick	subtraction
ruler	pi	square roots	
ellipse	place value	geometry	

1. What the acorn said when it grew up. _____

2. A person who's bad at grammar has this. _____

3. What Kull the Conqueror was called after he was knighted. _____

4. A dead parrot _____

5. How much your house costs. _____

6. What the tree developed after standing in a box all spring. _____

7. Something that has three feet but can't walk. _____

8. What the father did when his daughter wanted to go to summer camp. _____

9. What the man was when he got back from the beach. _____

10. What happens to a submarine when it breaks a leg. _____

11. This shape is never wrong. _____

12. What Jack Horner's thumb was covered with. _____

13. What the hairstylist who'd never colored anyone's hair was called. _____

14. A person in charge. _____

15. The only part that was left after the shark ate the moray eel. _____

16. What the mother told her son to put in the dishwasher. _____

17. If you support using farm equipment, you are this. _____

18. How Shakespeare often wrote his poetry. _____

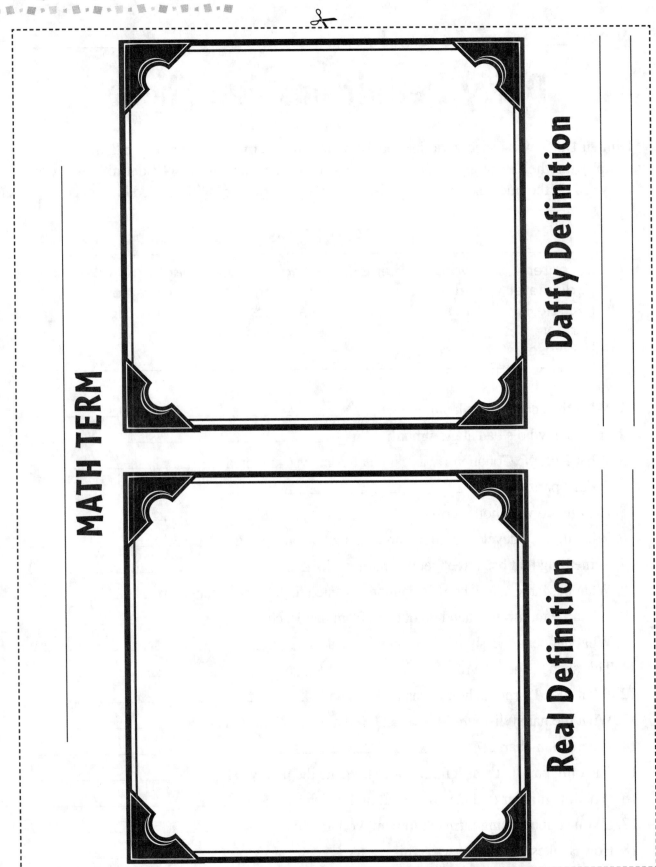

MATH TERM

Daffy Definition

Real Definition

The One-Minute Time Club

Challenge students to sharpen their basic math skills with the One-Minute Time Club.

Materials

Operations reproducibles (pages 54-57)
Star template (page 58)

Setting Up

◆ Section off part of a bulletin board with a strip of corrugated border. Add the title THE ONE-MINUTE TIME CLUB.

◆ Create a Time Club counter on a long strip of bulletin board paper. Draw a rectangle that stretches from the top of the strip to the bottom. Evenly divide the rectangle into 35 sections. At the top, write "Class Goal: 350 Math Stars."

Creating the Bulletin Board

◆ Explain to students that the One-Minute Math Club is an exercise to help them improve their math skills. To play, students must try to complete reproducible math sheets on the four basic operations in shorter amounts of time. For example, first they complete the addition sheet in 4 minutes, then 3 minutes, then 2 minutes, and finally 1 minute. Then they do this with subtraction, multiplication and division. When they correctly complete a math sheet, they receive a star. All of the students' stars are added to the class total. Once the class has earned a set amount of stars, they receive a special treat, such as a popcorn party or a day to play math games. (You'll need to figure out the goal for your class based on the number of students you have. As the operations become more difficult, fewer students will be able to reach the one-minute mark.)

◆ Every few weeks, give students an opportunity to take a One-Minute Time Club Test. Give each student a copy of the operation template they'll be completing. Place it face down in front of them and have them write their name and the amount of time they have to complete it at the top of the page.

◆ Have them begin filling out the worksheets while you keep time. After one minute call time for those students who had only one minute to complete the sheet. Call time again after two minutes, three minutes, and four minutes.

◆ Have the student exchange papers. Read the correct answers and have students write their score at the top of the page. Any student who answered all the problems correctly in the allotted time, receives a star to place on the bulletin board. Count up all the stars received and mark it on your class total.

The One-Minute Time Club Addition

Name _____

Time: _____

Score: _____

11 +7	2 +9	8 +7	7 +8		
6 +5	5 +9	12 +3	4 +4	5 +2	9 +8
6 +6	8 +3	5 +7	4 +12	3 +9	5 +5
6 +4	7 +7	6 +9	8 +4	7 +2	8 +5
3 +4	4 +5	5 +11	9 +3	8 +8	12 +6
7 +4	9 +9	3 +7	4 +9	8 +6	9 +5
5 +6	3 +3	6 +8	9 +7	4 +11	4 +7

25 Totally Awesome & Totally Easy Bulletin Boards
Scholastic Professional Books

The One-Minute Time Club Subtraction

Name _____

11 − 7	9 − 2	8 − 7	12 − 8

6 − 1	5 − 2	10 − 3	4 − 4	5 − 4	9 − 4
6 − 0	8 − 3	7 − 5	10 − 2	3 − 1	8 − 5
10 − 4	4 − 2	11 − 9	8 − 4	7 − 2	8 − 1
11 − 4	9 − 5	9 − 7	6 − 3	10 − 8	12 − 6
7 − 4	9 − 9	10 − 7	2 − 1	6 − 4	9 − 0
8 − 6	11 − 3	9 − 8	9 − 3	4 − 1	12 − 7

25 Totally Awesome & Totally Easy Bulletin Boards
Scholastic Professional Books

The One-Minute Time Club   Multiplication

Name _____

Time: _____

Score: _____

11 x 7	2 x 9	8 x 7	7 x 8		
6 x 5	5 x 9	12 x 3	4 x 4	5 x 0	9 x 8
6 x 6	8 x 3	10 x 7	4 x 12	3 x 9	5 x 5
6 x 1	7 x 7	6 x 9	8 x 4	7 x 2	8 x 5
3 x 4	4 x 5	5 x 11	9 x 3	8 x 8	12 x 6
7 x 4	9 x 9	0 x 7	4 x 9	8 x 6	9 x 5
5 x 6	3 x 10	6 x 8	9 x 7	1 x 11	4 x 7

25 Totally Awesome & Totally Easy Bulletin Boards
Scholastic Professional Books

Name _____

Time: _____

Score: _____

$77 \div 7 =$ $18 \div 9 =$ $56 \div 7 =$ $8 \div 8 =$

$30 \div 5 =$ $45 \div 9 =$ $36 \div 3 =$ $16 \div 4 =$ $50 \div 10 =$

$24 \div 8 =$ $24 \div 3 =$ $70 \div 7 =$ $48 \div 12 =$ $27 \div 9 =$

$6 \div 1 =$ $49 \div 7 =$ $59 \div 9 =$ $32 \div 4 =$ $14 \div 2 =$

$12 \div 4 =$ $20 \div 5 =$ $55 \div 11 =$ $27 \div 3 =$ $64 \div 8 =$

$28 \div 4 =$ $81 \div 9 =$ $42 \div 7 =$ $36 \div 9 =$ $48 \div 6 =$

$6 \div 6 =$ $30 \div 10 =$ $48 \div 8 =$ $63 \div 7 =$ $99 \div 11 =$

25 Totally Awesome & Totally Easy Bulletin Boards
Scholastic Professional Books

Name: _____

Addition

Time: _____

Name: _____

Multiplication

Time: _____

Name: _____

Subtraction

Time: _____

Name: _____

Division

Time: _____

25 Totally Awesome & Totally Easy Bulletin Boards
Scholastic Professional Books

Bulls and Bears

Students learn about the stock market by tracking stock prices for ten weeks—and also practice working with decimals and fractions.

Materials

business section of the newspaper
   (one day a week for ten weeks)
Portfolio Balance Sheet
   reproducible (page 60)
paper in assorted colors

Setting Up

♦ Cover the bulletin board with the stock market section of the newspaper. For more visual interest, staple the sections at different angles. Create a banner titled BULLS AND BEARS. Under the title, staple the headings "Week 1" through "Week 10."

Creating the Bulletin Board

♦ Explain to students that they will be learning about the stock market by selecting five stocks for a portfolio and then tracking the stocks for ten weeks. Share with students copies of the stock market page from the newspaper. Discuss all of the information listed on the page and point out that the column labeled "Last" lists the price for one share of that company's stock at the end (or close) of the day. This is the column they will be working with.

♦ Show them how to convert the fractional cost of each share of stock to a decimal. Demonstrate how they can multiply a fictional amount of shares by the decimal number to determine how much money the stock is worth. (For instance, if they own 50 shares of a stock priced at $38.125 per share, they own $1,906.25 worth of that stock.)

♦ Break the class into groups of four or five students. Each group should select five stocks for their portfolio. They can determine how much they want to spend on each stock, but they cannot spend more than $50,000 total. They should record the number of shares of stock they own in the five companies they picked and track the investments over the course of the next ten weeks.

♦ On the same day each week, one student from each group should bring in the business section of the newspaper. Groups should then calculate the growth or decline in value of the five stocks they have selected and add the totals together. (They can use the Portfolio Balance Sheet.) Then have each group write their group number and their total portfolio value on a different color paper. Post each group's portfolio values on the bulletin board. Because each group's portfolio values are color-coded it is easy for everyone to track the rankings of the groups and to see how the values change over the course of the ten-week period.

Bulls and Bears Portfolio Balance Sheet

Enter the information for each of the five stocks your group owns. Calculate the values of each item and then add the totals together to find your total portfolio value.

GROUP: _____

WEEK: _____

Stock Name	Number of shares	Price per share	Value of stock*
1.			
2.			
3.			
4.			
5.			
Total Portfolio Value:			

* To calculate the value of your stock, multiply the number of shares you own by the price per share.

GROUP: _____

WEEK: _____

Stock Name	Number of shares	Price per share	Value of stock*
1.			
2.			
3.			
4.			
5.			
Total Portfolio Value:			

* To calculate the value of your stock, multiply the number of shares you own by the price per share.

25 Totally Awesome & Totally Easy Bulletin Boards
Scholastic Professional Books

Getting Into Shape

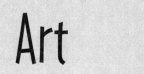

Students discover the shapes all
around them with an artful activity.

Materials

Artist's Sketchbook reproducible (page 62)   magazines   a bowl of fruit (optional)
color comics from the Sunday newspaper   how-to draw books

Setting Up

♦ Cover the bulletin board with the Sunday comics. Add the title Getting Into Shape.

Creating the Bulletin Board

♦ Locate a few how-to draw books at your local or school library. The majority of them describe
how artists, whether drawing figures, landscapes, or still life, will first break the objects down
into geometric shapes. A good book to try is Mona Brookes' *Drawing with Children.* Share the
books with students.

♦ Pass out copies of the Artist's Sketchbook to your students. On the left side, have students draw
the geometric core of a figure, still life, or landscape. On the right side, they should redraw the
geometric core and then complete the drawing, adding details, shading, and color.

♦ Choose any of the following activities as the basis for students' work:

—Pair up the students. One student will strike a pose that he or she can hold for a few minutes
while the other student draws the basic shapes of the figure in the left-hand space. They can
then switch. After both students have completed the left side, they can complete the drawing on
the right.
—Have the students push their desks into a circle. Place a large still life, such as a bowl of fruit,
on a table in the center of the circle. Students should draw the still life from their own perspective, starting with the geometric core. This activity produces similar pictures but each one has a
slightly different perspective.
—Let students look through magazines to find an image to use for their work.
—Take students outside so they can draw a landscape.

♦ Invite students to share their work with the class before you display the work. Post students'
work on the bulletin board.

FINISHED DRAWING

BASIC SHAPES

Snapshots of the Year

Wrap up the school year with a bulletin board that reflects the year's highlights.

Materials

Snapshot template (page 64)

Setting Up

♦ Cover your board with bulletin-board paper—any color will work. Create a title strip that reads SNAPSHOTS OF (your grade level) and staple it to the bulletin board. For an extra touch, write each letter in the title inside a snapshot frame and staple it to the bulletin board.

Creating the Bulletin Board

♦ Write the letters A to Z on the blackboard or down the left side of a large sheet of chart paper.

♦ As a class, brainstorm all of the activities, units, field trips, assemblies, and events of the past school year that begin with each letter.

♦ Decide which item from each list best represents the grade's experience.

♦ Ask each student to select one item or topic to illustrate and describe. Pass out copies of the Snapshot template to the class. Students should draw a detailed picture of their topic in the snapshot frame. On the top line of the template, students should write the upper- and lower-case letter for their topic and the name of their topic. On the lines below, students can write a short paragraph about the topic.

♦ Collect the completed snapshots and hang them in alphabetical order on the bulletin board. This activity is a wonderful way for the students to reflect on all that has happened over the past year.

♦ You can also use this bulletin board as a culminating activity for any major unit.

Snapshots of the Year Snapshot template

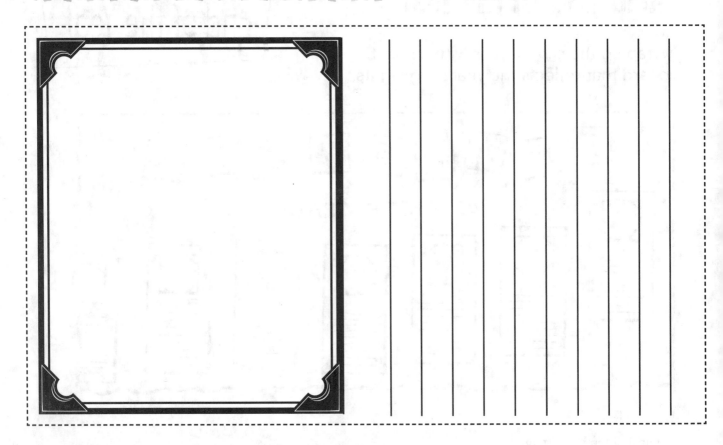

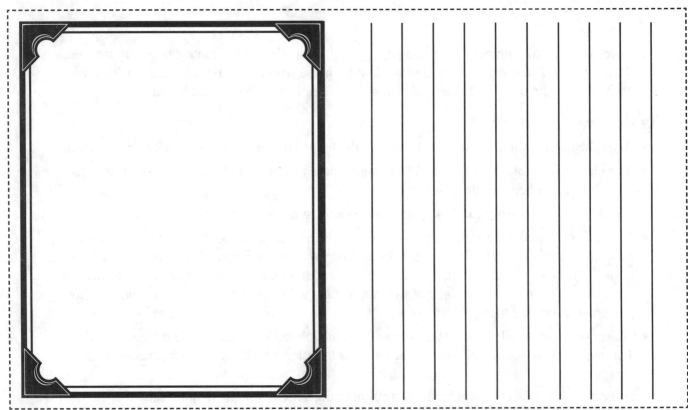

25 Totally Awesome & Totally Easy Bulletin Boards
Scholastic Professional Books